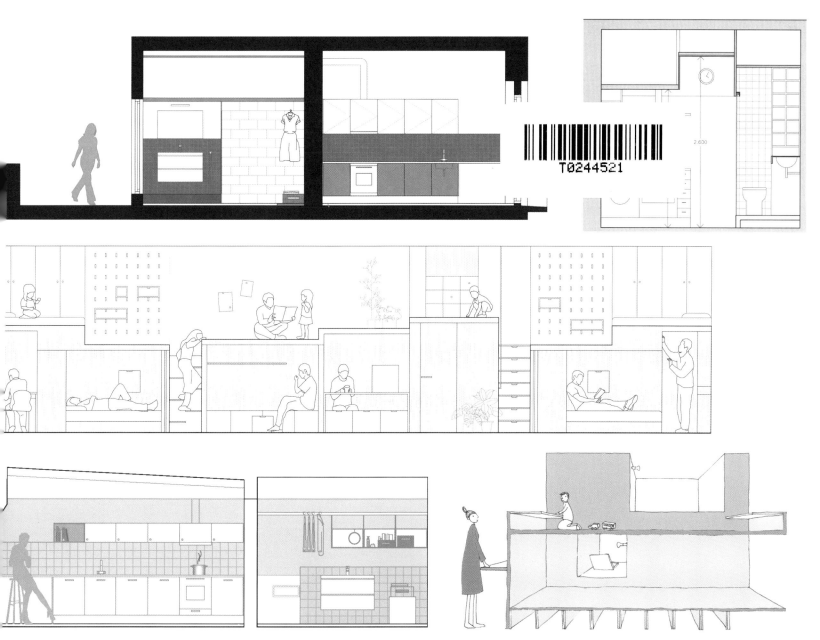

Modular Tiny Apartment Plans

© 2021 Instituto Monsa de ediciones.

First edition in April 2021 by Monsa Publications,
Gravina 43 (08930) Sant Adrià de Besós.
Barcelona (Spain) T +34 93 381 00 93
www.monsa.com monsa@monsa.com

Editor and Project Director Anna Minguet
Layout Eva Minguet
(Monsa Publications)
Printing Gómez Aparicio

Shop online:
www.monsashop.com

Follow us!
Instagram: @monsapublications
Facebook: @monsashop

ISBN: 978-84-17557-31-7
D.L. B 4231-2021
April 2021

MODULAR
TINY APARTMENT
PLANS

monsa

ADAPTATION & SPACE SAVING

The new urban housing projects usually have a lower number of square feet than a few years ago, and also seeks to reduce costs and optimize the available space. Normally the tendency is to unify the dining, living room and kitchen in the same environment, and the elimination of internal partitions to give spaciousness and allow more natural light.

Los nuevos proyectos de vivienda urbana disponen por lo general de un número inferior de metros cuadrados que hace algunos años, y además se busca reducir costes y optimizar el espacio disponible. Normalmente la tendencia es unificar comedor, sala de estar y cocina en un mismo ambiente, así como la eliminación de tabiques interiores para dar sensación de amplitud y permitir una mayor entrada de luz natural.

DESIGNING
THE SPACE OF A COMPACT DWELLING

Designing the space of a compact dwelling requires to prioritize the needs of its inhabitants and adapt them to their physical, legal and budgetary constraints. The goal is to create spaces that improve the quality of life of its inhabitants and project their personality. In order to achieve it, minimalist solutions such as open plants to unify spaces with complementary roles are used; also the predominance of straight lines and pure forms, or the preference of monochromes and light colors on the walls. As well as using the minimum necessary furniture for not filling the space and get the housing looks wider, with ideas for hidden or concealed storage, and so on.

Diseñar el espacio de una vivienda compacta exige priorizar las necesidades de sus habitantes y conciliarlas con sus limitaciones físicas, legales y de presupuesto. El objetivo es crear espacios que mejoren la calidad de vida de sus habitantes y proyecten su personalidad. Para conseguirlo, se emplean soluciones minimalistas como el recurso de plantas abiertas para unificar espacios con funciones complementarias; el predominio de la línea recta y las formas puras, o la preferencia por las monocromías y colores claros en las paredes. Así como empleando el mínimo mobiliario necesario para no llenar el espacio y conseguir que la vivienda parezca más amplia, con ideas para almacenamientos ocultos o disimulados, etc.

USE
THE STAIRS YOU NEED
TO MAKE THE MOST OUT OF
EVERY OPTION

If you have compact living space, you need to make the most out of every option, and that includes your stairs You can use this space to improve your storage by building shelves and drawers. This helps to manage things easily.

Si se dispone de un espacio habitable y compacto, se debe aprovechar al máximo cada opción, y eso incluye sus escaleras. Es fundamental usar este espacio para mejorar su almacenamiento construyendo estantes y cajones. Esto ayuda a administrar las cosas fácilmente.

When it comes to fit in in a compact space, remember that ceiling is your limit. There is a lot you can do here. You can add more railing or shelves, or even use storage boxes. Make it your storage space for stuff you don't need very often. The point is, look around, and make the most of what you have.

Cuando se trata de adaptar un espacio compacto, el techo es el límite. Hay muchas cosas que se pueden hacer aquí. Pueden agregarse más barandillas o estantes, o incluso usar cajas de almacenamiento. Convertirlo en un espacio de almacenamiento para objetos no tan necesarios.

MODULAR FURNITURE
THAT CAN BE FOLDED, NESTED
AND RETRACTED
FOR EASY HANDLING

Modular furniture that can be folded, nested and retracted for easy handling. In addition to storing, the storage solutions serve to clear and divide the space. Built-in or freestanding, open or closed, the possibilities are endless, but the most important thing is that they are adapted to our needs and to the objects that they have to store or display. Storage is most efficient when it is customized to suit the occupants' habits. In small spaces, the most ingenious storage ideas create the ideal environment for each space.

Los muebles modulares pueden doblarse, anidarse y contraerse para facilitar su manipulación. Además de guardar, las soluciones de almacenamiento sirven para liberar y dividir el espacio. Integrados o independientes, abiertos o cerrados, las posibilidades son infinitas, pero lo más importante es que se adapten a nuestras necesidades. El almacenamiento es más eficiente cuando se personaliza a los hábitos de los ocupantes. En espacios reducidos, las ideas más ingeniosas de almacenamiento consiguen un ambiente idóneo para cada espacio.

A ROOM LOOKS
BEAUTIFUL WITH MODULAR FURNITURE

A room looks beautiful and modern with modular furniture. They create a better storage system and make our life fully functional. Modular furniture is usually prefabricated and used according to the space of the room.

Los muebles modulares convierten a una habitación en moderna y hermosa. Crean un mejor sistema de almacenamiento y hacen de nuestra vida algo totalmente funcional. Los muebles modulares suelen ser prefabricados y se utilizan de acuerdo con el espacio de la habitación.

THINK VERTICALLY,
AND THE WALLS WILL BECOME OUR
BEST ALLIES

When we find ourselves with small spaces, the main idea is to think vertically and look for additional storage spaces. The walls become our best ally, they not only serve to hang images and mirrors, but also to create and invent new spaces that help us live more comfortably.

Cuando nos encontramos con espacios reducidos, la principal idea es pensar en vertical y buscar espacios de almacenamiento adicional. Las paredes se convierten en nuestro mejor aliado, no solo sirven para colgar imágenes y espejos, sino para crear e inventar nuevos espacios que nos ayuden a vivir más cómodamente.

FLEXIBILITY TO ADAPT
TO NEW HOME
WORKING
METHODS

Teleworking is already part of our lives, it is the new working method implemented. With the help of modular furniture, we can adapt all kinds of spaces without the need for major changes, and also very economically.

El teletrabajo ya forma parte de nuestras vidas, es el nuevo método de trabajo implantado. Con la ayuda de muebles modulares, podemos adaptar todo tipo de espacios sin necesidad de grandes cambios, y además de forma muy económica.

INDEX

NANLUOGUXIANG HUTONG | 258 sq ft

B.L.U.E. ARCHITECTURE STUDIO
www.b-l-u-e.net
Team: Shuhei Aoyama, Yoko Fujii, Yufeng Di, and Hanlin Yang
Beijing, China
Photo © Ruijing Photo

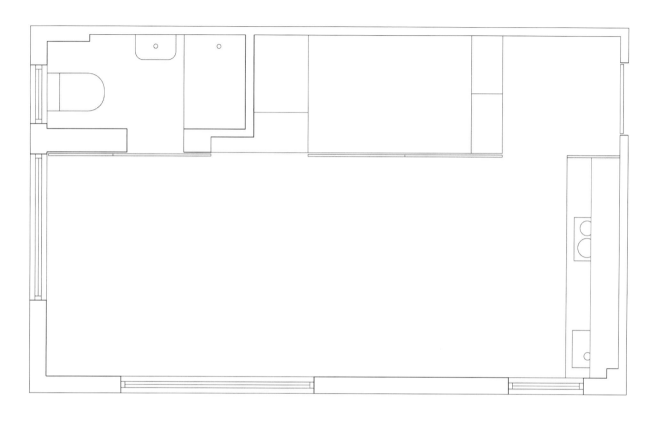

Floor plan

DENGSHIKOU HUTONG RESIDENCE | 463 sq ft

B.L.U.E. ARCHITECTURE STUDIO

www.b-l-u-e.net
Team: Shuhei Aoyama, Yoko Fujii, and Lingzi Liu
Beijing, China
Photo © Ruijing Photo

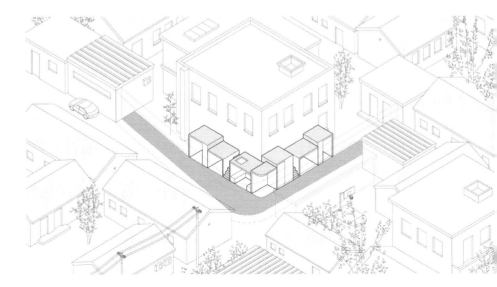

Conceptual diagram

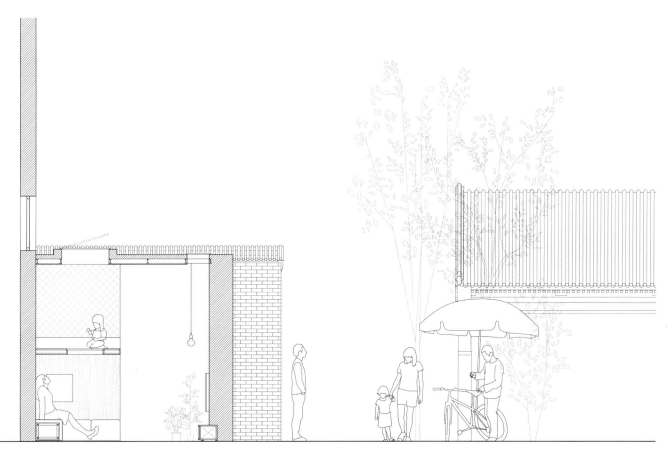

Building sections

Section

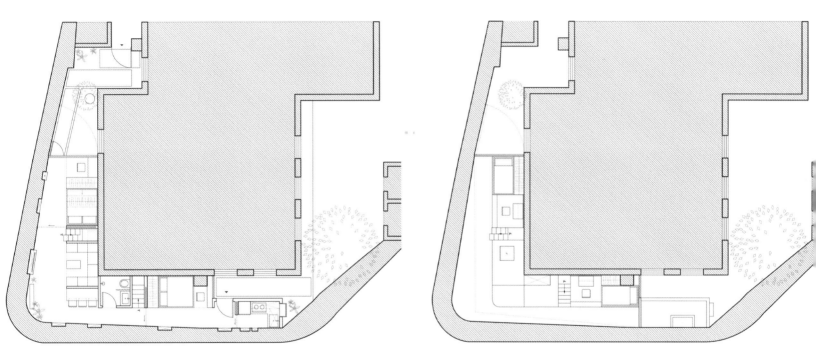

Ground floor plan

Second floor plan

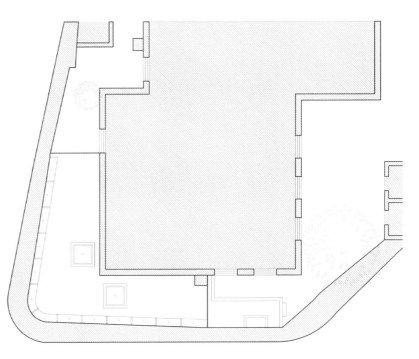

Roof plan

LIVING SPACE | 516 sq ft

RUETEMPLE
www.ruetemple.ru
Team: Alexander Kudimov, Daria Butakhina, and Evgeny Dagaev
Moscow, Russia
Photo © Ruetemple and NTV Broadcasting Company

Longitudinal section

Cross section

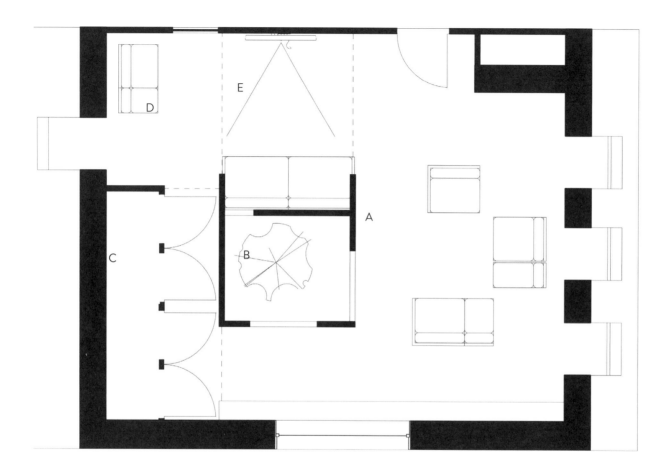

Floor plan

A. Living area
B. Relaxation area
C. Storage
D. Lounge
E. TV area

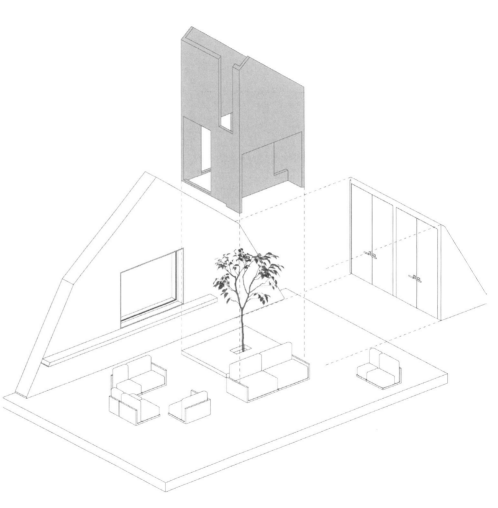

Axonometric view

MOORMANN'S KAMMERSPIEL | 441 sq ft

NILS HOLGER MOORMANN AND B&O GROUP

www.moormann.de

Prototype

Photo © Julia Rotter

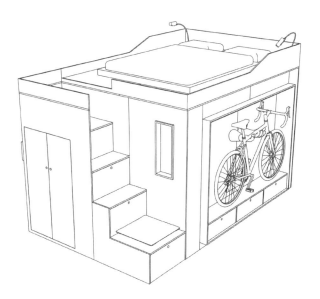

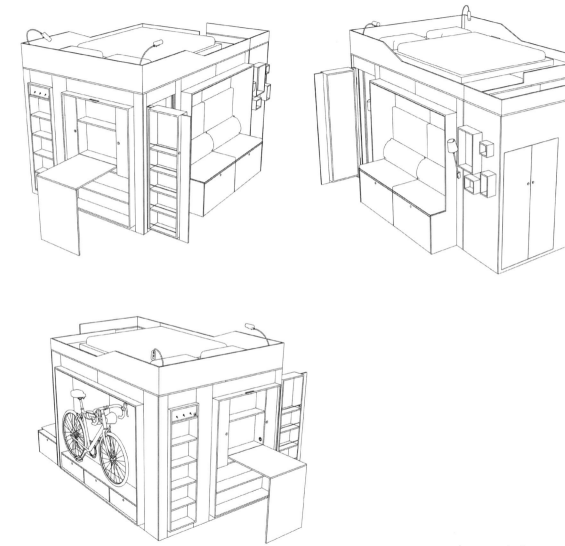

Axonometric views

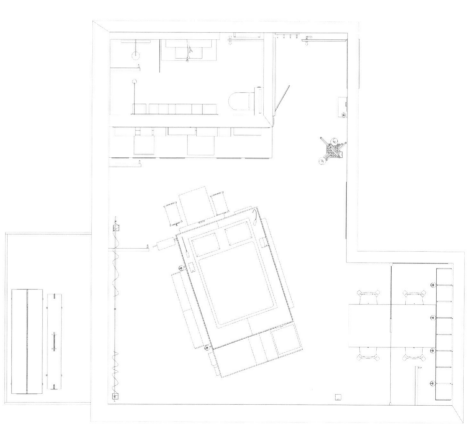

Floor plan

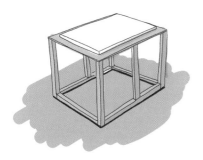
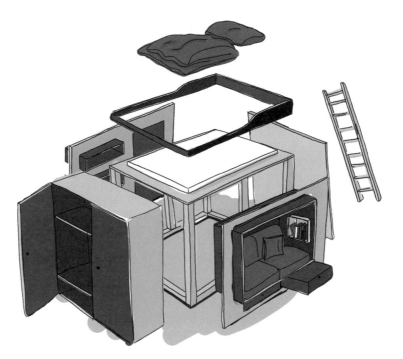
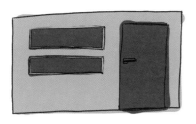

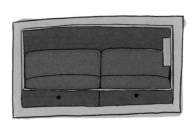

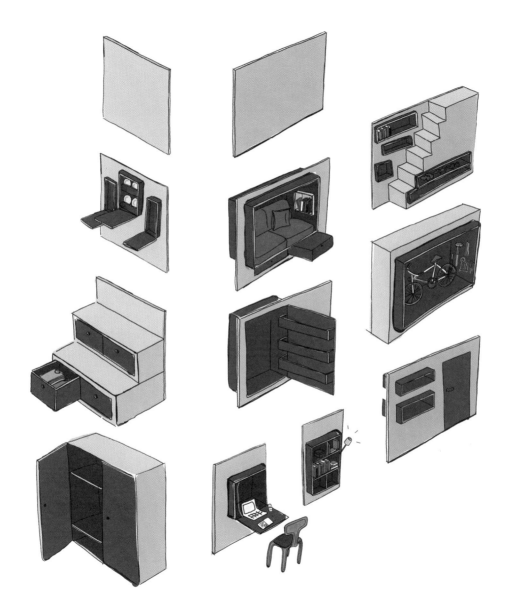

Design development sketches

A GRAPHIC REFURBISHMENT BY THE SEA | 430 sq ft

TIAGO DO VALE ARQUITECTOS

www.tiagodovale.com
Team: Tiago do Vale, María Cainzos Osinde, Hugo Quintela, and Louane Papin
Caminha, Portugal
Photo © João Morgado

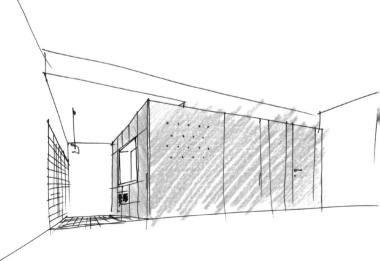

Design development sketch

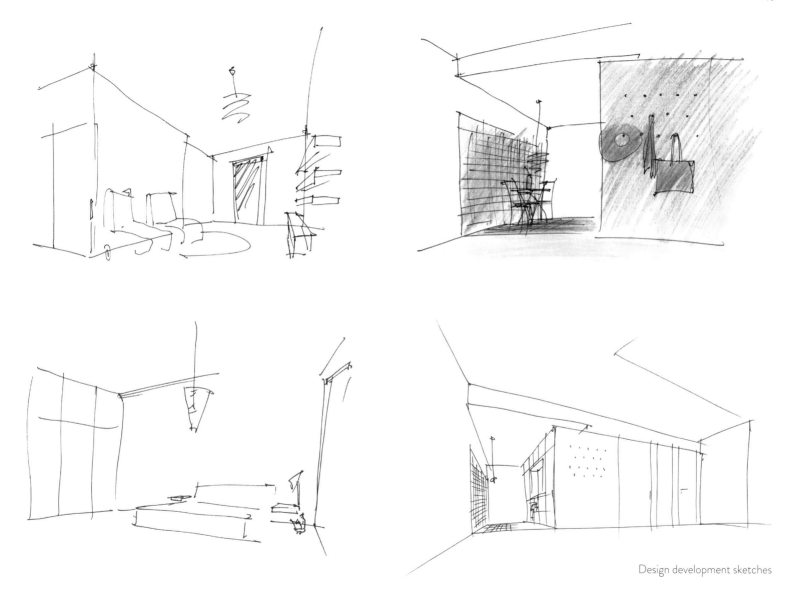

Design development sketches

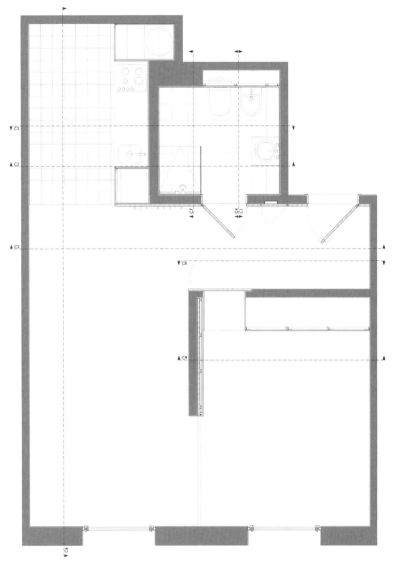

Floor plan

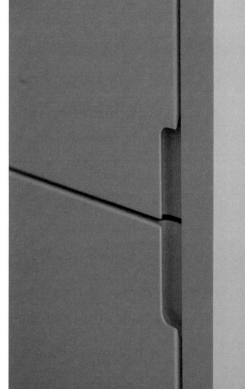

Section C8

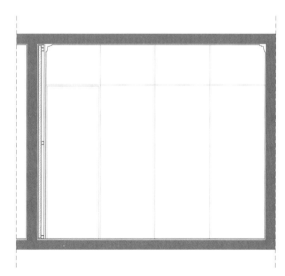

Section C9

Section 9 (closed doors)

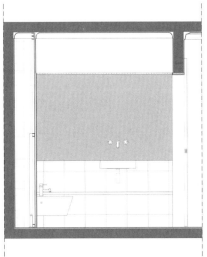

Section C1

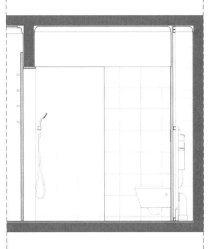

Section C4

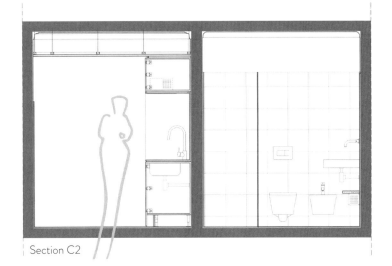

Section C2

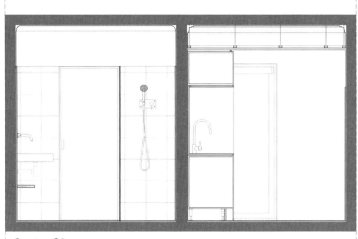

Section C3

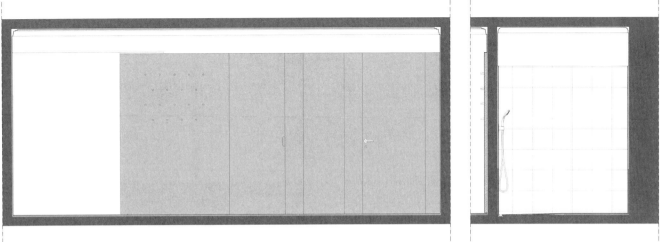

Section 5

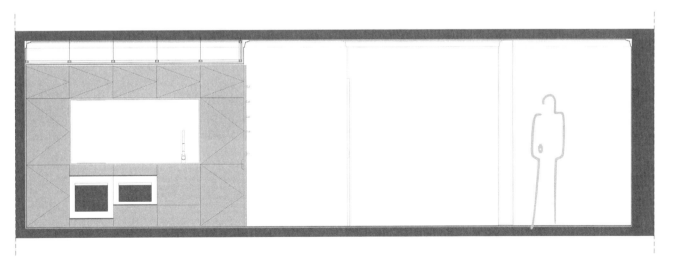

Section C6

FLAT 8 | 549 sq ft

DESIGN EIGHT FIVE TWO
www.designeightfivetwo.com
Team: Norman Ung
Hong Kong, SAR China
Photo © Hazel Yuen Fun

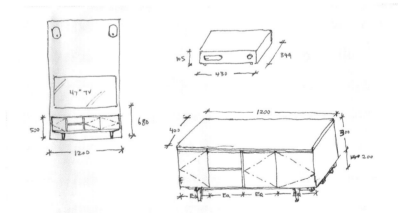

Conceptual design sketch

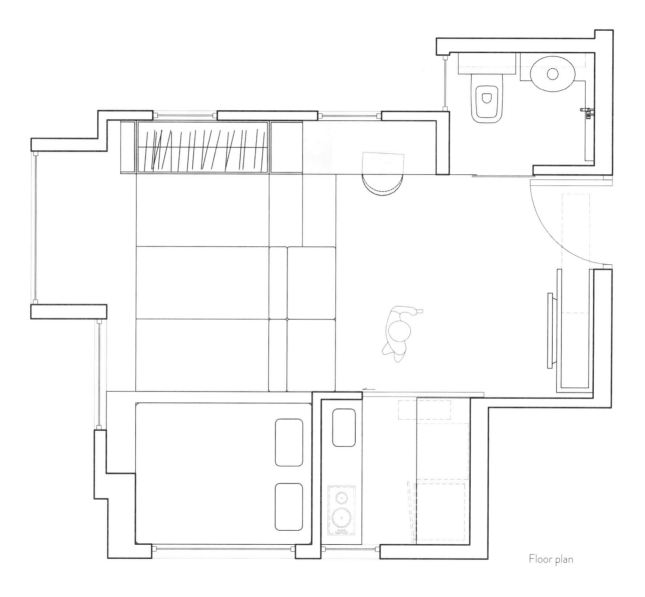

Floor plan

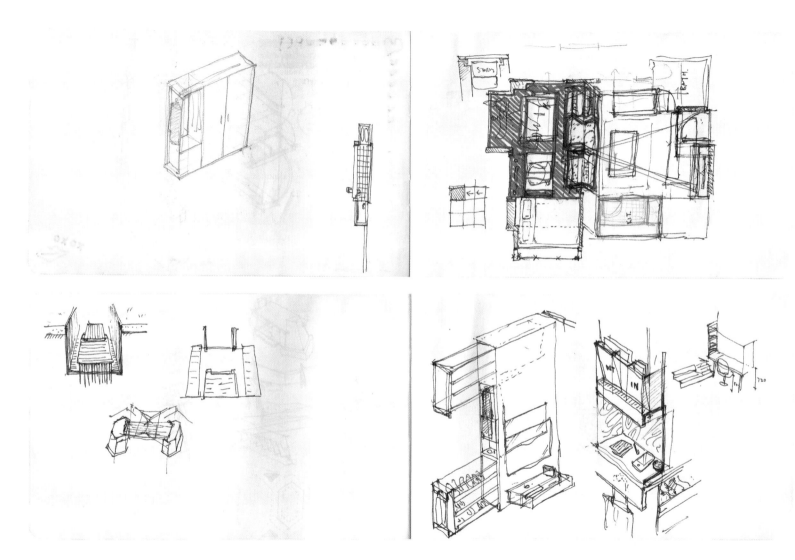

Conceptual design sketches

NANLUOGUXIANG HUTONG | 258 sq ft

B.L.U.E. ARCHITECTURE STUDIO
www.b-l-u-e.net
Team: Shuhei Aoyama, Yoko Fujii, Yufeng Di, and Hanlin Yang
Beijing, China
Photo © Ruijing Photo

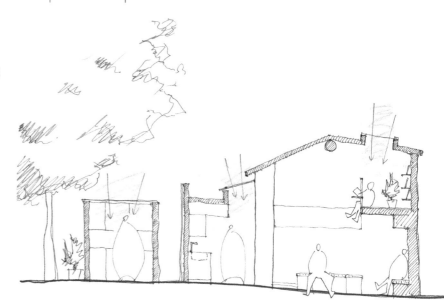

Design development sketch

Design development sketches

Building section

Design development sketch

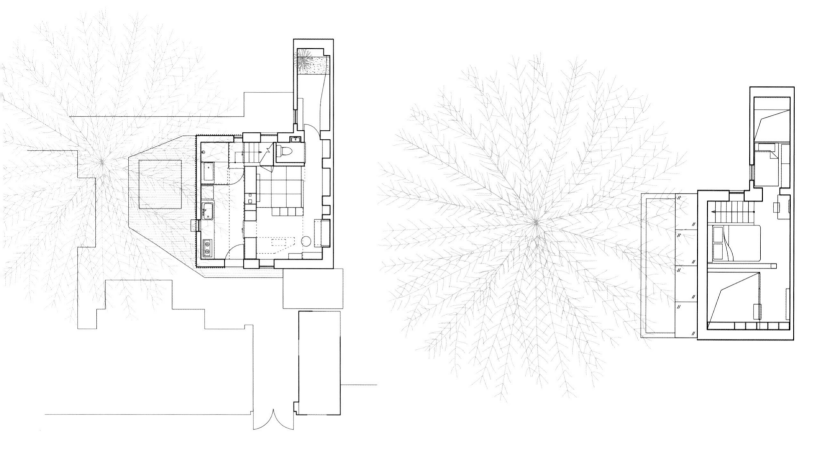

Ground floor plan

Second floor plan

LONG ESTATE | 323 sq ft

MILI MLODZI LUDZIE

www.milimlodziludzie.com
Team: Przemysaw Nowak, and Lech Moczulski
Poznan, Poland
Photo © PION - piondaily.tumblr.com

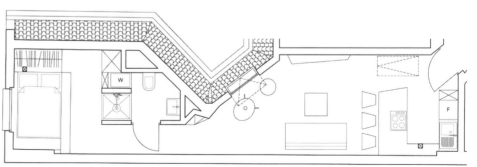

Floor plan

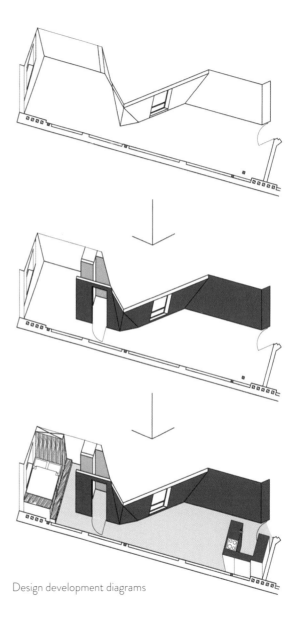

Design development diagrams

BRANDBURG HOME AND STUDIO | 398 sq ft

MODE:LINA
www.modelina-architekci.com
Team: Pawel Garus, Jerzy Wozniak, and Kinga Kin
Poznan, Poland
Photo © Patryk Lewinski

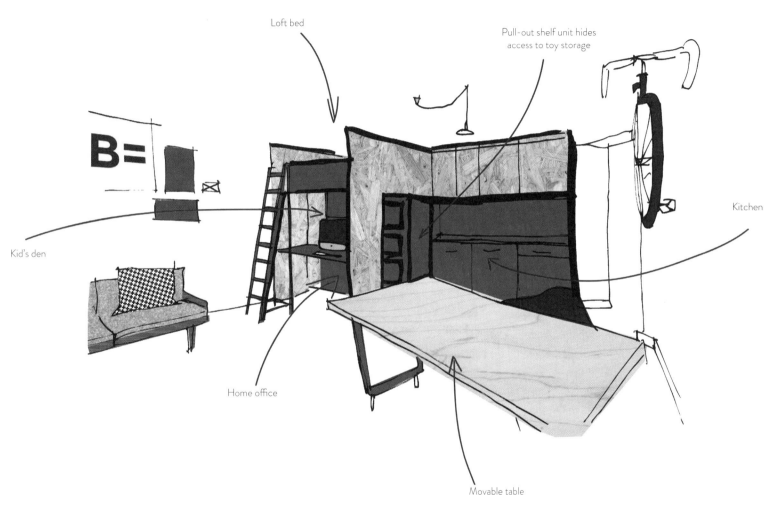

Loft bed

Pull-out shelf unit hides
access to toy storage

Kitchen

Kid's den

B=

Home office

Movable table

Schematic design

PETER'S APARTMENT | 280 sq ft

MILI MODZI LUDZIE
www.milimlodziludzie.com
Team: Przemysaw Nowak, and Lech Moczulski
Poznan, Poland
Photo © Lusia Kosik

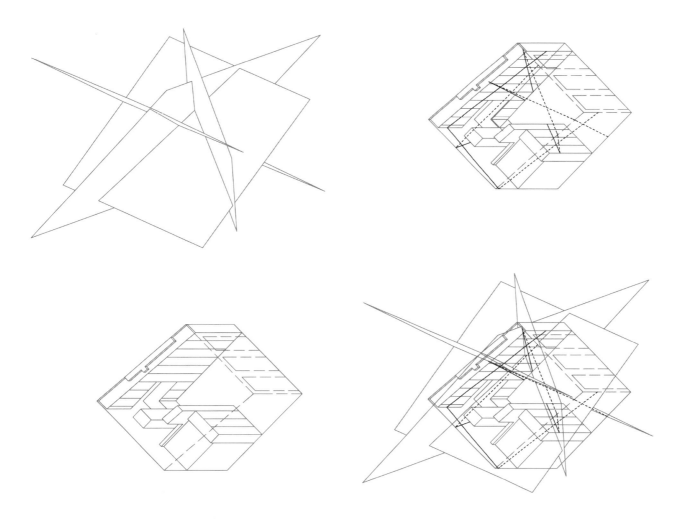

Ideogram

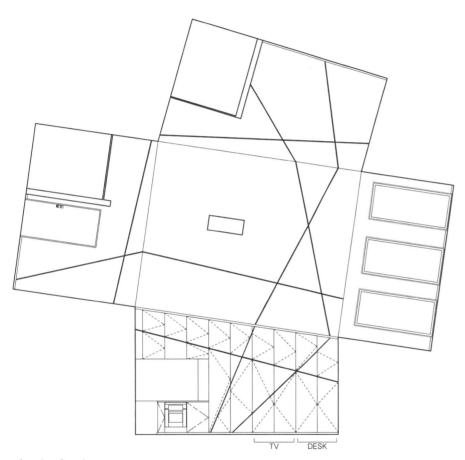

TV　DESK

Interior elevations

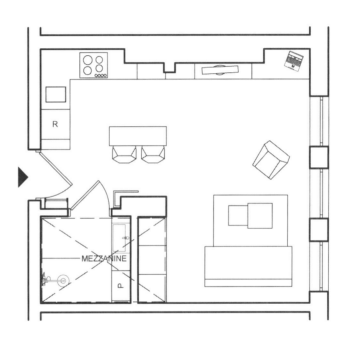

MEZZANINE

R

P

10   100
0 50   200

Floor plan

KOWLOON BAY | 269 sq ft

DESIGN EIGHT FIVE TWO
www.designeightfivetwo.com
Team: Norman Ung, Peter Lampard, Ryan Lam,
Hazel Fun Yuen, and Tony Lai
Hong Kong, SAR China
Photo © Hazel Yuen Fun, Dennis Cheung

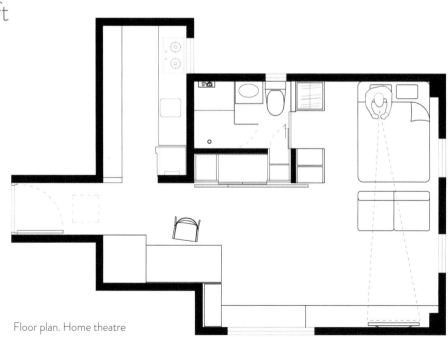

Floor plan. Home theatre

Floor plan. Space for relaxation

Floor plan. Dining table as desk

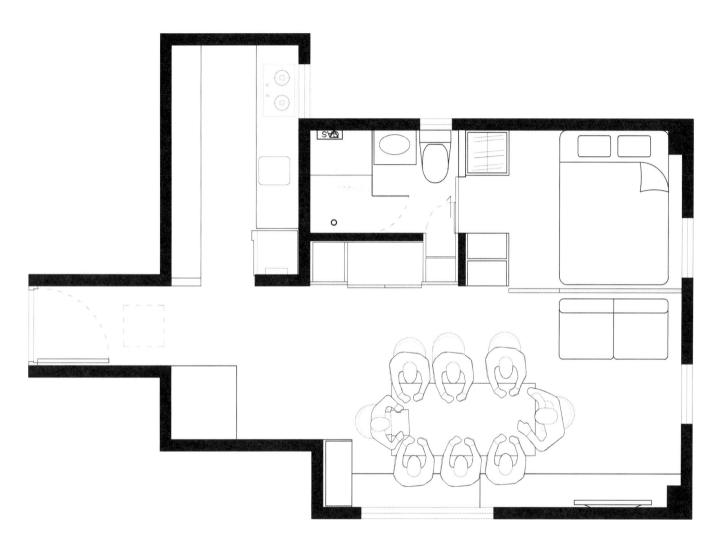

Floor plan. Dining area expansion

THE WHITE RETREAT | 387 sq ft

COLOMBO AND SERBOLI ARCHITECTURE

www.colomboserboli.com
Sitges, Spain
Photo © Roberto Ruiz
www.robertoruiz.eu

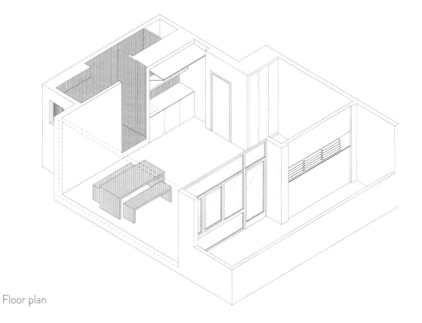

Floor plan

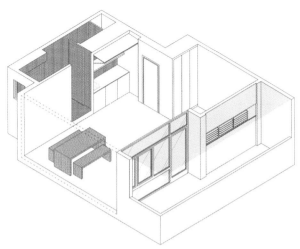

Terrace

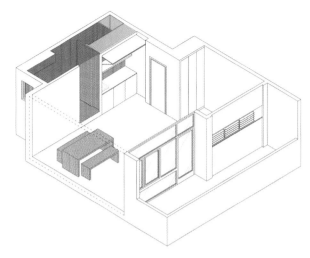

Bathroom / kitchen

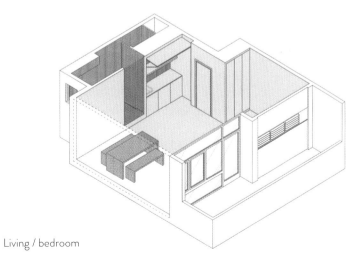

Living / bedroom

BRERA APARTMENT | 366 sq ft

CESARE GALLIGANI, PLANAIR

www.planairstudio.com

Team: Danilo Monzani, Mert Bokurt, and Andrea Zammataro

Milan, Italy

Photo © Luca Broglia

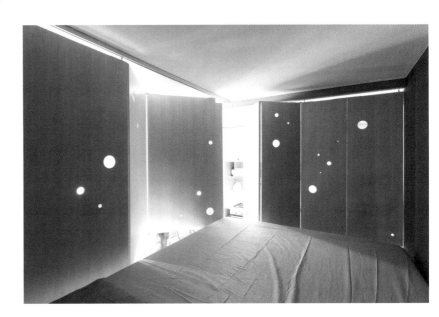

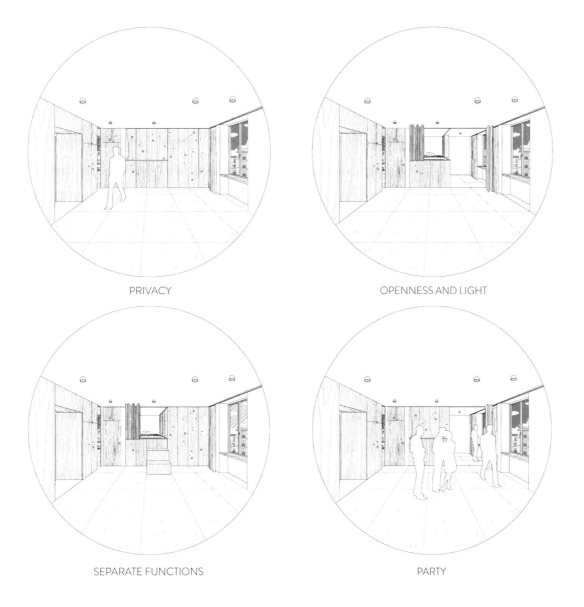

PRIVACY

OPENNESS AND LIGHT

SEPARATE FUNCTIONS

PARTY

Perspective views

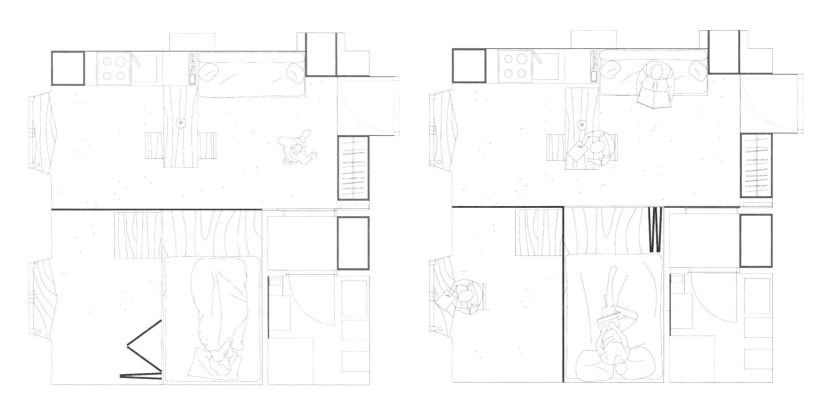

Floor plan for sleeping

Floor plan for working

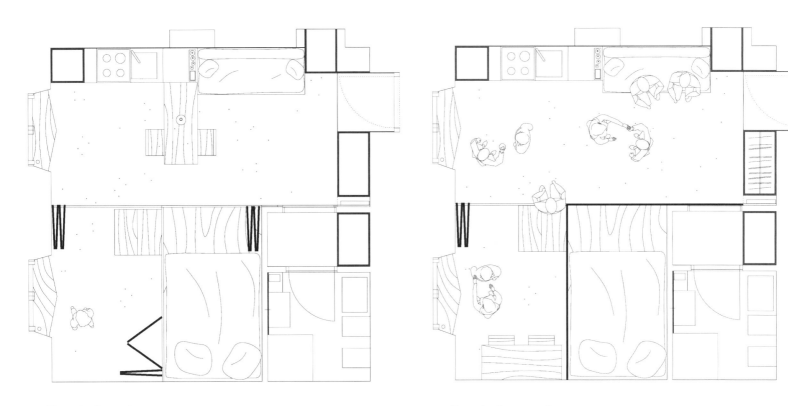

Floor plan for maximum space

Floor plan for entertainment

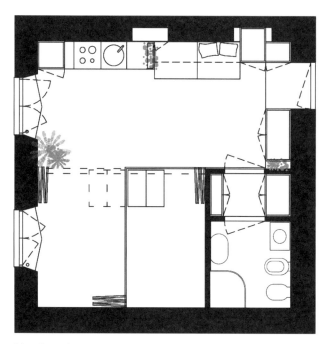

New floor plan

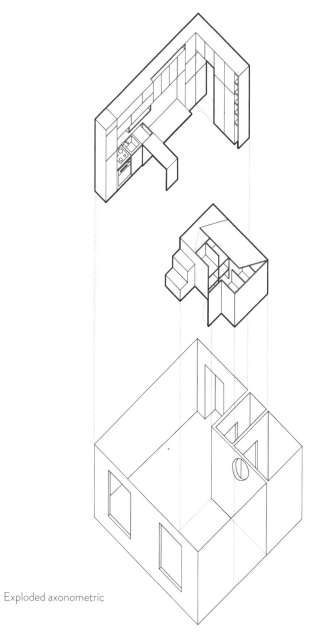

Exploded axonometric

Bed wardrobe axonometric view

APARTMENT IN TOKYO | 769 sq ft

NAOTO MITSUMOTO & NAOKO HAMANA
www.mihadesign.com
Tokyo, Japan
© Sadao Hotta

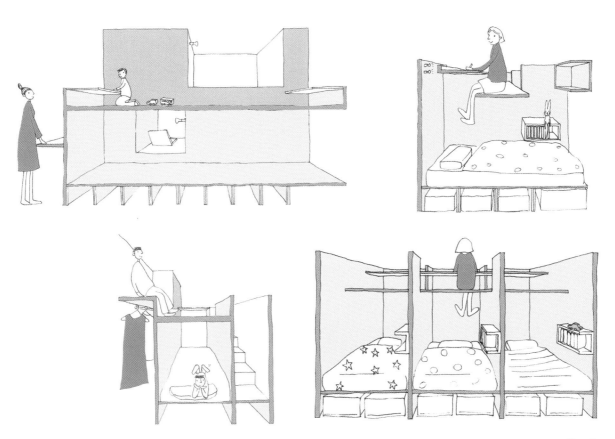

Sketches

Floor plan

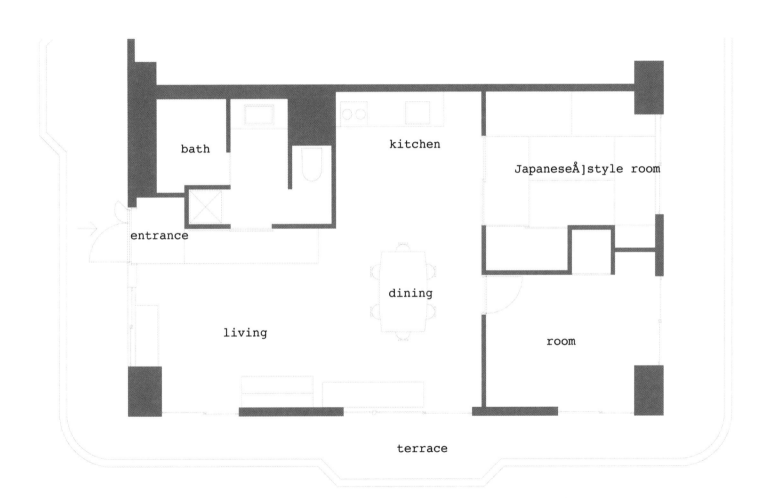

bath

kitchen

Japanese-style room

entrance

dining

living

room

terrace

BEDROOM BETWEEN TWO VOLUMES | 538 sq ft

ECDM – EMMANUEL COMBAREL DOMINIQUE MARREC
www.ecdm.eu
Mountrouge, France
© Gaston Bergeret

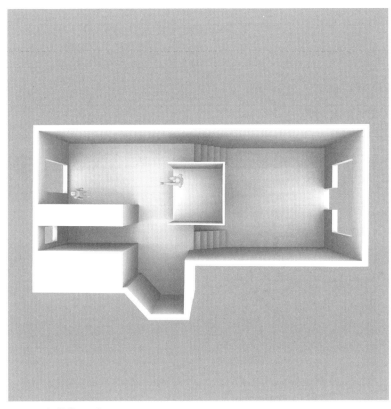

3-D floor plan

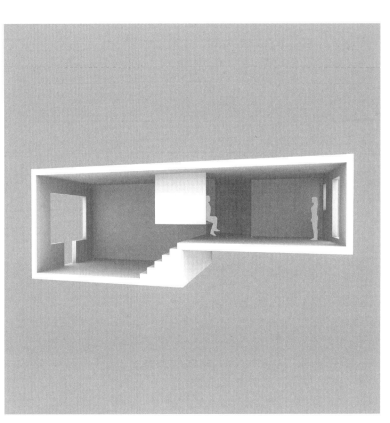

3-D longitudinal section

ULTRATINY APARTMENT | 172 sq ft

JULIE NABUCET | MARC BAILLARGEON

www.julienabucet.com
www.marcbaillargeon.net
Paris, France
© Sylvie Durand

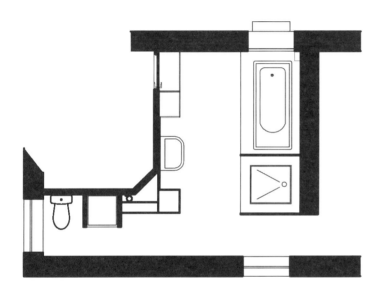

Floor plan before renovation

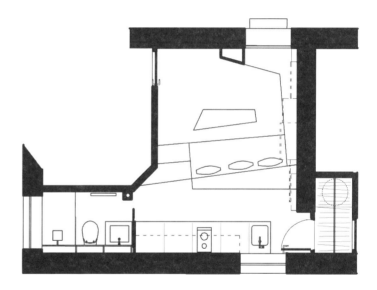

Floor plan after renovation

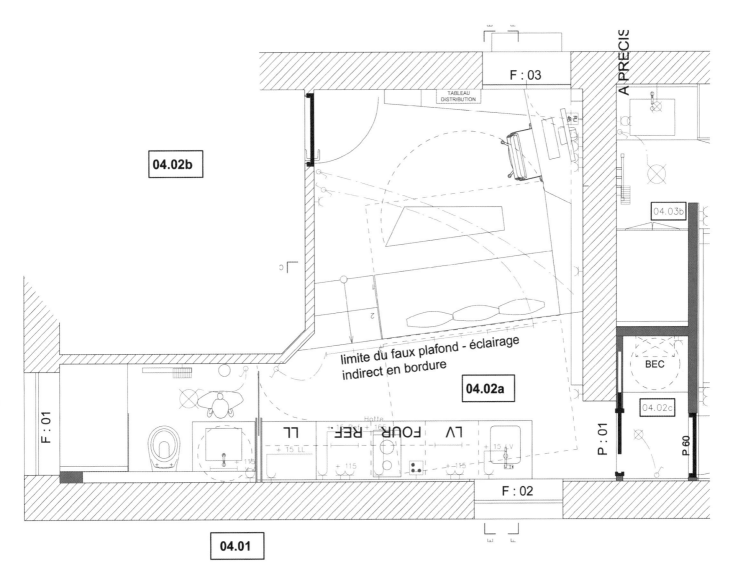

CASA ALMIRANTE | 215 sq ft

MYCC_ OFICINA DE ARQUITECTURA
www.mycc.es
Madrid, Spain
© Elena Almagro
www.elenaalmagro.com

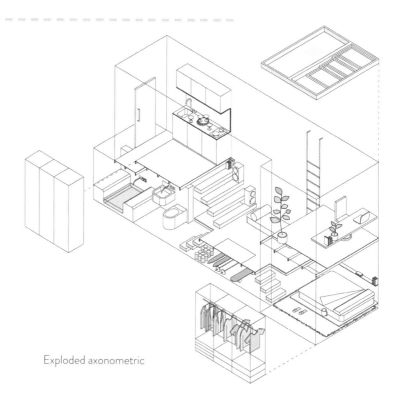

Exploded axonometric

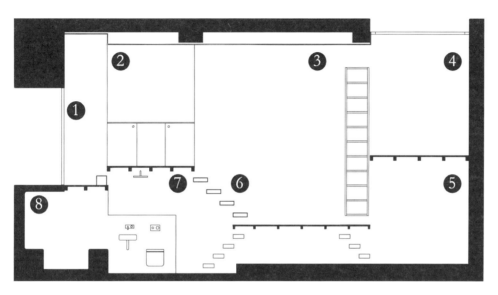

Floor plan

1. Access high

2. Walk through kitchen 3. Kind of living

4. Light chill out

5. Office bedroom

6. Contemplative stands

7. XL bathroom

8. Hammann

SANTA CATERINA | 258 sq ft

LOIS LOEDA

www.loisloeda.com
Barcelona, Spain
© Lois Loeda

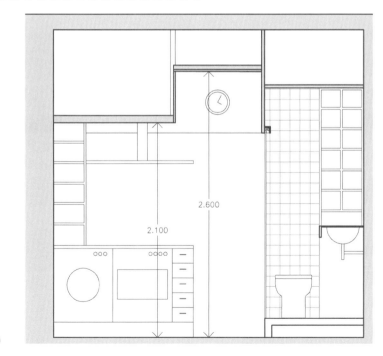

Kitchen and bathroom section

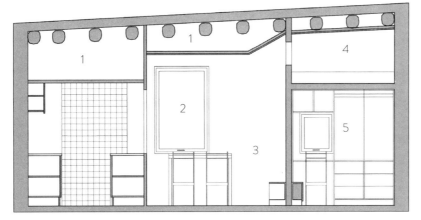

1. Reachable boxroom
2. Dining room
3. Living room
4. Bedroom
5. Dressing room

E

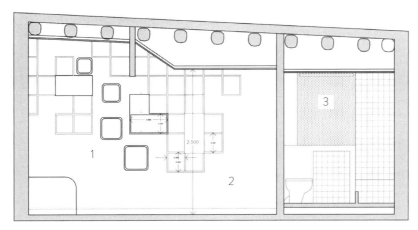

1. Living room
2. Library
3. Bathroom

H

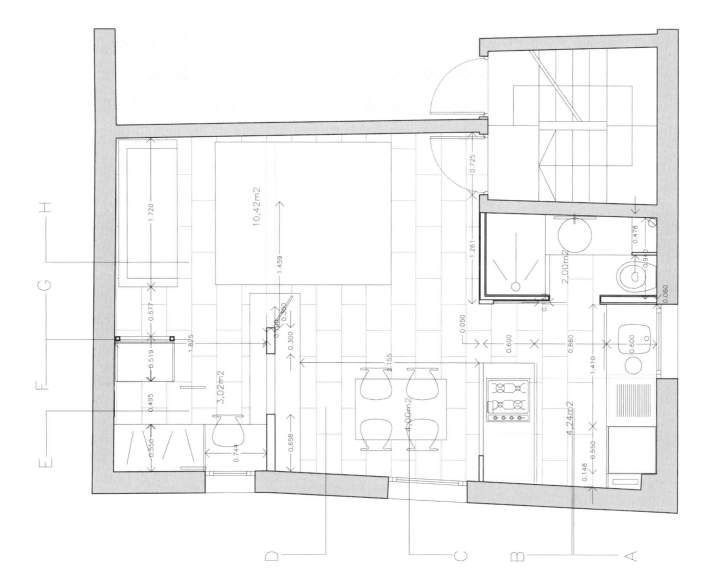

H

G

F

E

10.42m2

3,02m2

4,00m2

2,00m2

4,24m2

1.720

1.459

0.577

0.519

1.825

0.495

0.550

0.744

0.658

0.300

2.155

0.600

0.860

0.600

1.410

0.550

0.148

1.261

0.725

0.050

0.478

0.940

0.060

D

C

B

A

NADODRZE APARTMENT | 312 sq ft

3XA
www.3xa.pl
Cracow, Poland
© 3XA

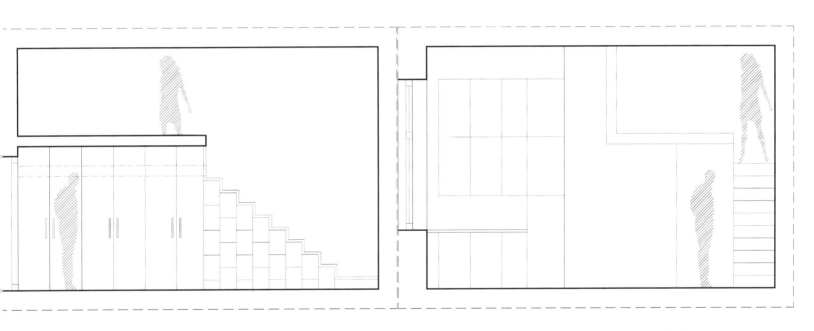

Sections

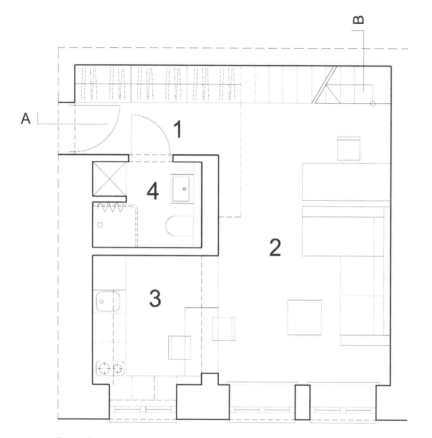

Floor plan

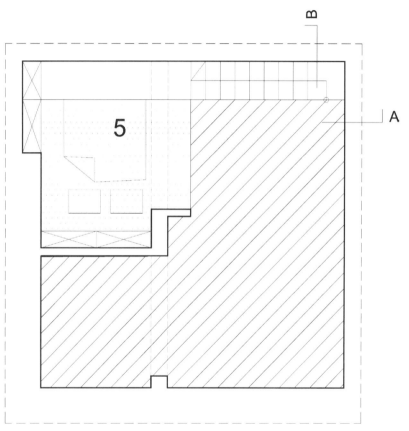

5

B

A

Floor plan

CASA ROC | 376 sq ft

NOOK ARCHITECTS

www.nookarchitects.com

Barcelona, Spain

© Nieve - Audiovisial producer

Bedroom and living room elevation

0   0.5   1   2.5 m

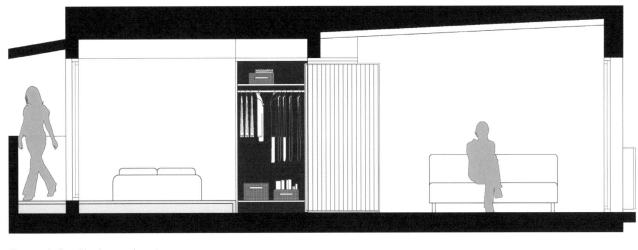

Entrace hall and bedroom elevation

0   0.5   1   2.5 m

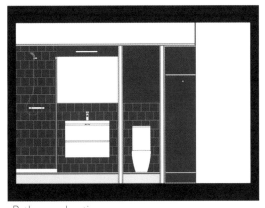

Bathroom elevation

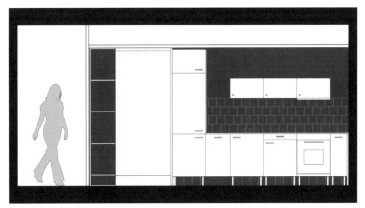

Kitchen elevation

0   0.5   1   2.5 m

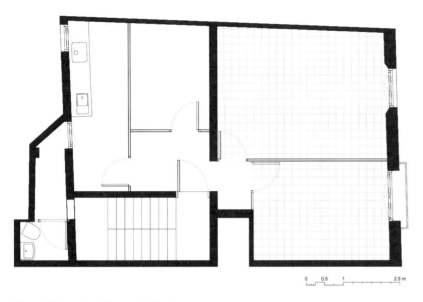

Ground floor plan before rehabilitation

0   0.5   1   2.5 m

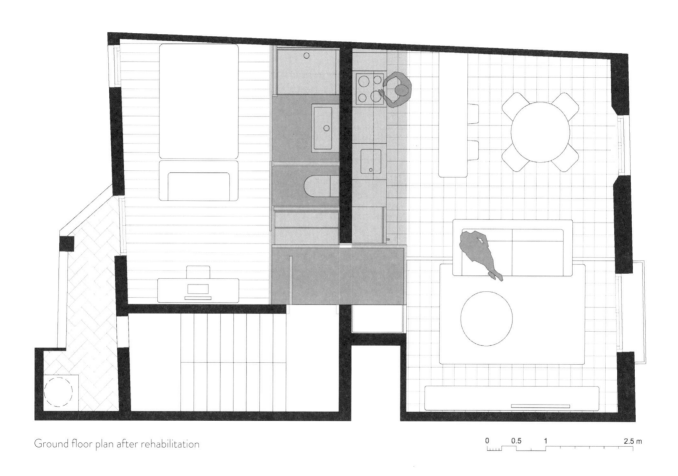

Ground floor plan after rehabilitation

0   0.5   1   2.5 m

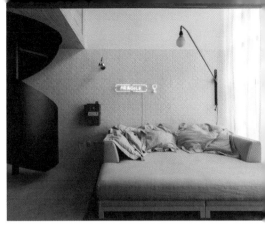

AP 1211 | 376 sq ft

ALAN CHU
www.chu.arq.br
Sao Paulo, Brazil
© Djan Chu

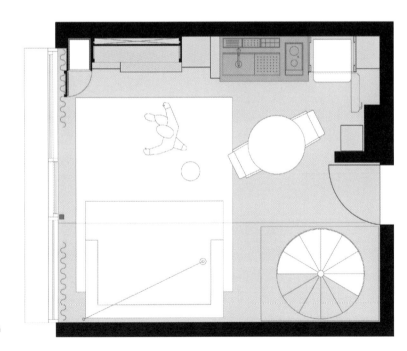

Ground floor plan

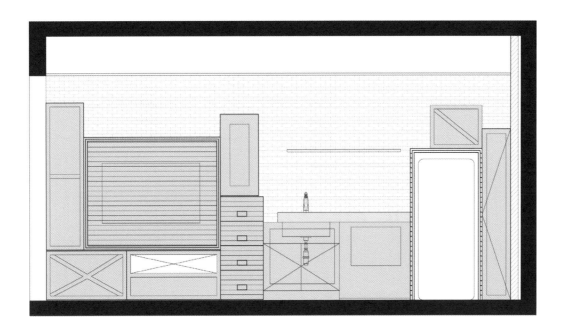

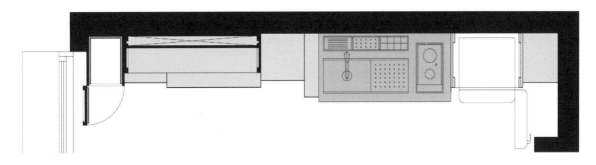

Main room's section and plan

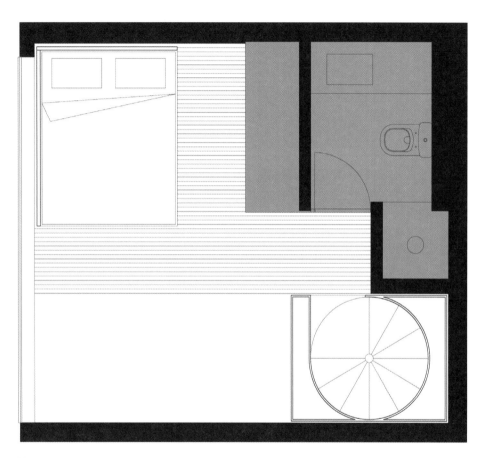

Mezzanine

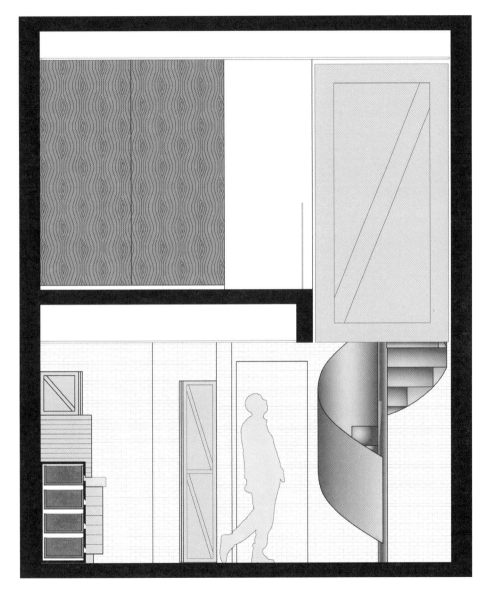

Section

UNIFOLDING APARTMENT | 400 sq ft

MICHAEL CHEN & KARI ANDERSON

www.normalprojects.com
Ney York, USA
© Alan Tansey

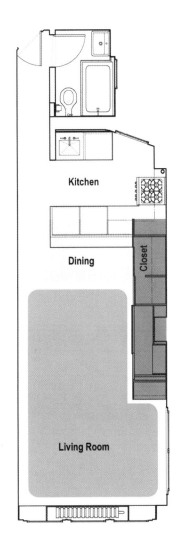

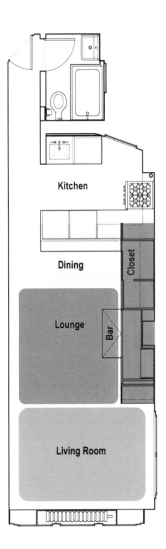

Floor plan

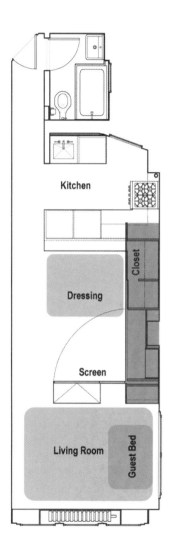

Kitchen

Dressing

Closet

Screen

Living Room

Guest Bed

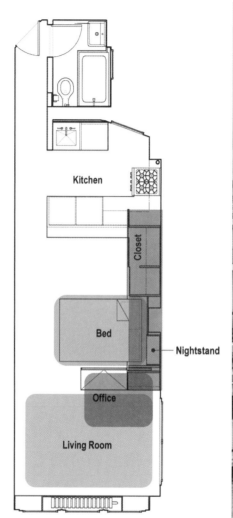

Kitchen

Closet

Bed

— Nightstand

Office

Living Room

Floor plan

TWIN HOUSE | 409 sq ft

NOOK ARCHITECTS

www.nookarchitects.com

Barcelona, Spain

© Nieve - Audiovisial producer

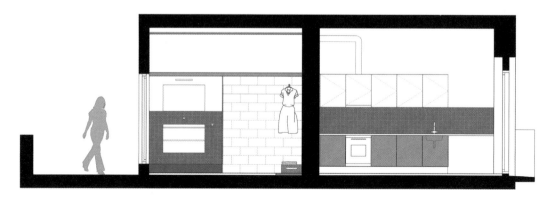

Twin 1 section

0   0.5   1   2.5 m

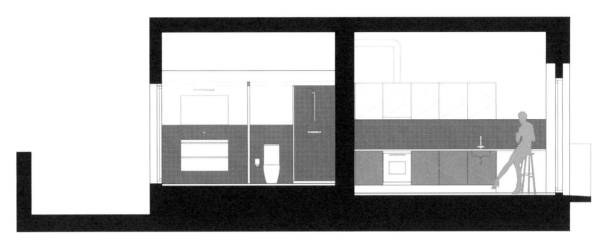

Twin 1 section. West area

0   0.5   1   2.5 m

Section. Twin 2 at left

0   0.5   1   2.5 m

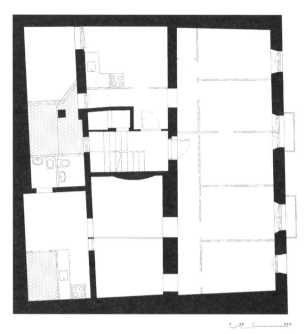

Ground floor plan before rehabilitation

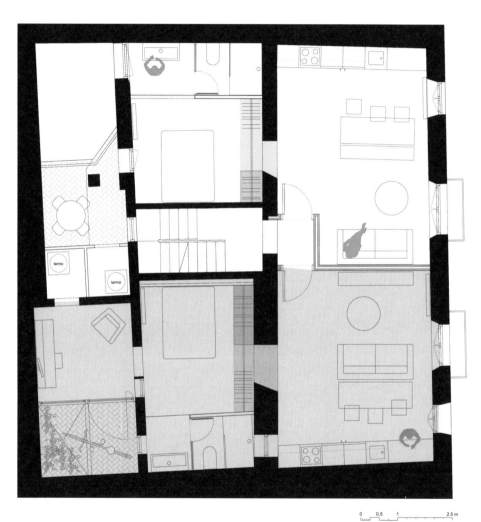

Ground floor plan before rehabilitation.
The colored area belongs to the second apartment of 355,212 ft

AWKWARD APARTMENT | 425 sq ft

SPECHT HARPMAN
www.spechtharpman.com
Ney York, USA
© Specht Harpman

3D section

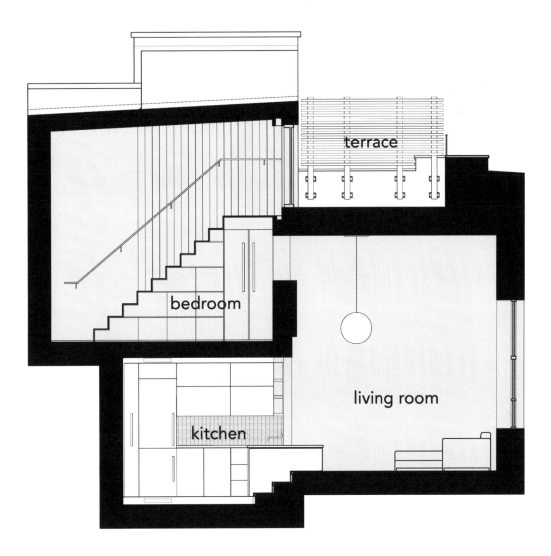

terrace

bedroom

kitchen

living room

Section

bathroom

kitchen

stairwell

living room

Floor plan

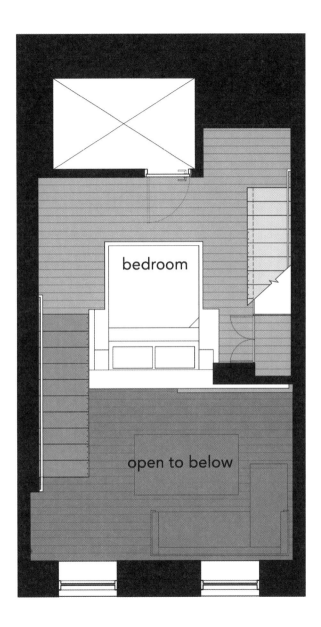

bedroom

open to below

Floor plan

ROC3 | 430 sq ft

NOOK ARCHITECTS
www.nookarchitects.com
Barcelona, Spain
© Nieve - Audiovisial producer

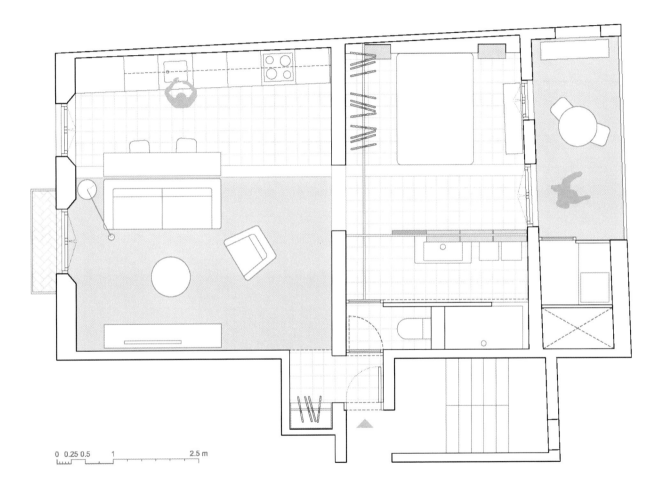

0 0.25 0.5   1   2.5 m

Floor plan

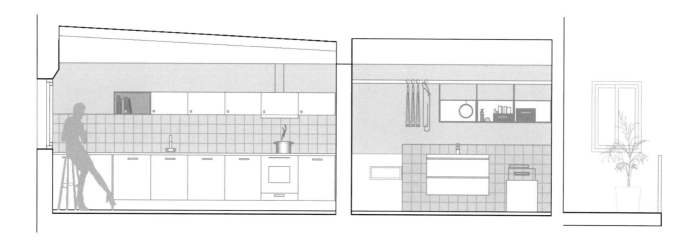

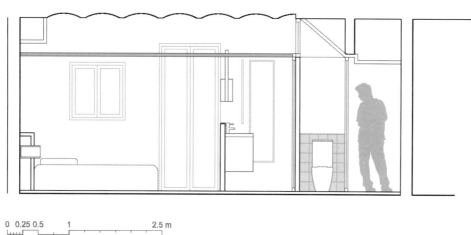

0 0.25 0.5   1   2.5 m

Sections

M HOUSE | 689 sq ft

SINATO ARCHITECTS
www.sinato.jp
Team: Chikara Ohno
Kanagawa, Japan
Photo © Toshiyuki Yano

Perspective view

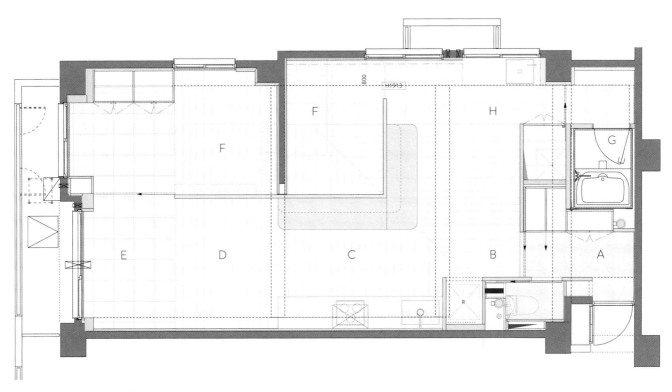

Floor plan

A. Entry
B. Living area
C. Kitchen
D. Dining area
E. Area for relaxation
F. Bedroom
G. Bathroom
H. Washroom
I. Storage
J. Toilet room

360 DEGREE FLAT | 430 sq ft

SFARO ARCHITECTS
www.sfaro.co.il
Tel-Aviv, Israel
© Boaz Lavi & Jonathan Blum

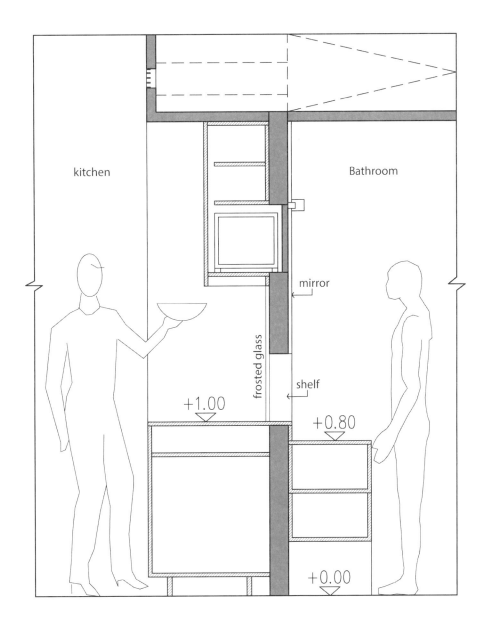

kitchen

Bathroom

mirror

frosted glass

shelf

+1.00

+0.80

+0.00

Section

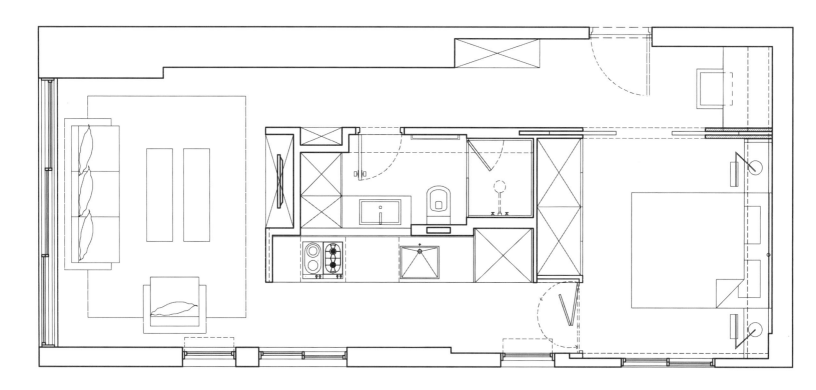

Floor plan

MOUNTAIN SHELTER | 269 sq ft

BEIROT, BERNARDINI ARCHITECTS
www.beriotbernardini.net
Navacerrada, Spain
© Yen Chen

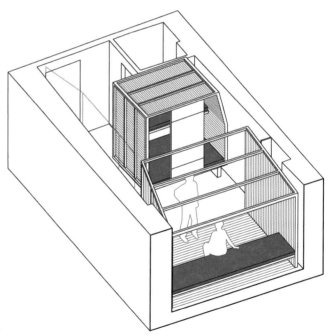

Living

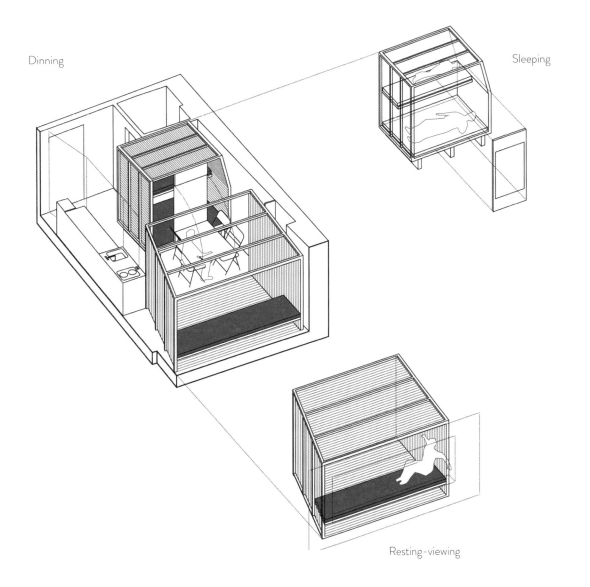

Dinning

Sleeping

Resting-viewing

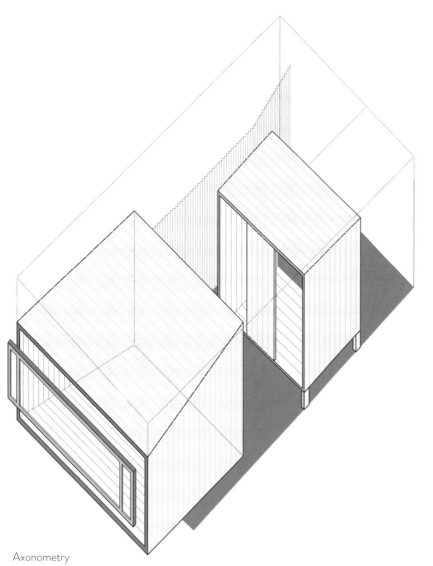

Axonometry

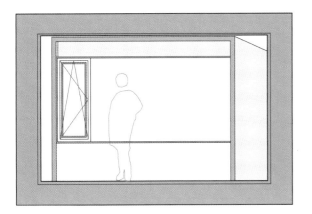

Cross section

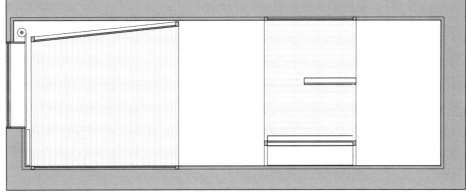

Longitudinal section

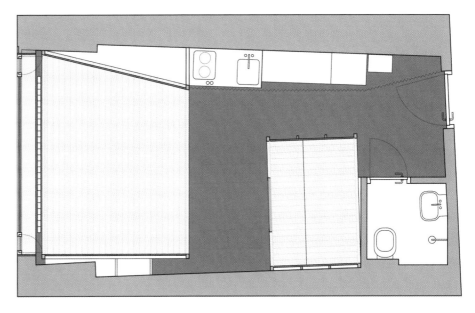

Floor plan

SHELTER IN THE RAVAL | 409 sq ft

EVA COTMAN

www.evacotman.com
Barcelona, Spain
© Eva Cotman, Maria Ceballos

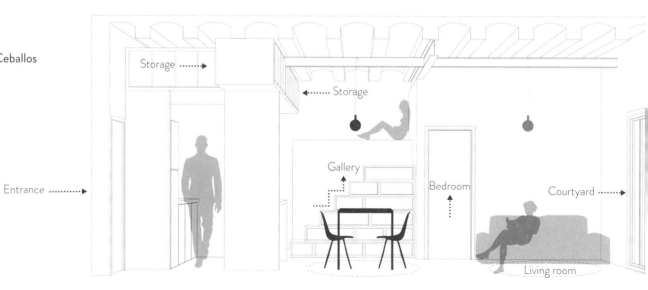

Storage ┈┈┈▶

◀┈┈┈ Storage

Gallery

Entrance ┈┈┈┈▶

Bedroom

Courtyard ┈┈┈┈▶

Living room

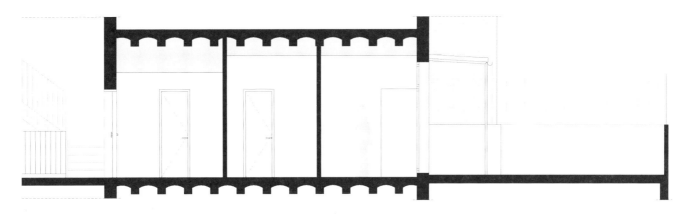

Section before rehabilitation

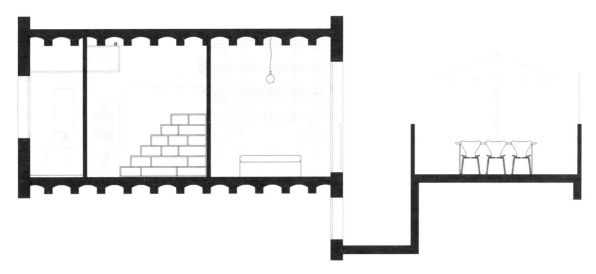

Section after rehabilitation

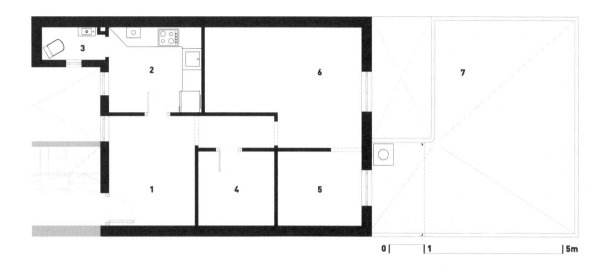

Ground floor plan before rehabilitation

1. Entrance

2. Kitchen

3. Bathroom

4. Bedroom

5. Dining room

6. Living room

7. Courtyard

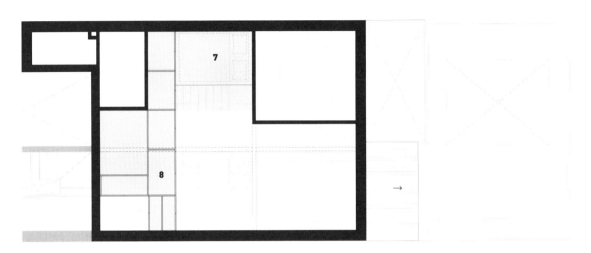

Gallery after rehabilitation

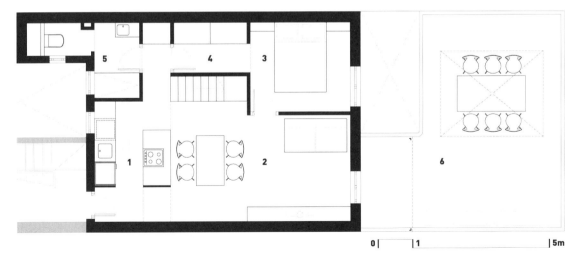

Floor plan after rehabilitation

1. Kitchen

2. Dining and living room

3. Bedroom

4. Wardrobe

5. Bathroom

6. Patio

7. Gallery with the guests bed

8. Built-in storage

0 | | 1 | 5m

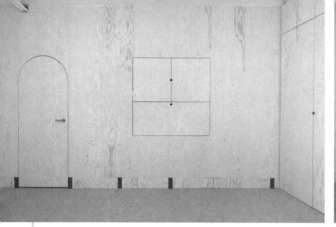
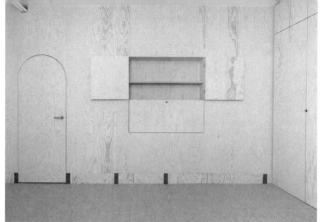

INHABITED WOODEN WALLS | 603 sq ft

AURÉLIE MONET KASISI
www.monetkasisi.ch
Carpenter: Fabien Pont
Geneva, Switzerland
Photo © Yann Laubscher

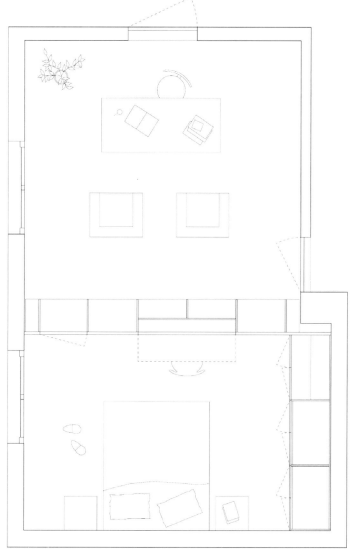

Office and au pair bedroom floor plan

Home cinema and playroom floor plan

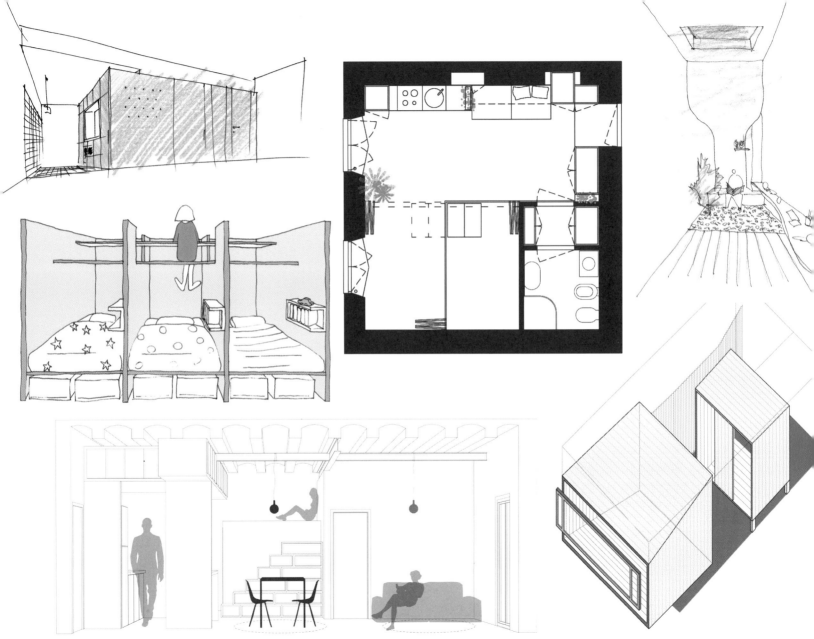